Ultimate
Armenian Cookbook

TOP 111 Traditional Armenian Recipes You Can Cook Right Now!

by

Slavka Bodic

Why This Cookbook?

I was born in the Balkans. I used to live in former Yugoslavia, and I currently reside in Serbia. While growing up in Yugoslavia, we were mostly exposed to the Soviet Union, but Moldova, Armenia, or Georgia weren't well-known for us. However, I tasted excellent Armenian food even in that period and I fell in love with it. After the fall of Communism and the dissolution of both the Soviet Union and Yugoslavia, new countries got an opportunity to increase the visibility of their national cuisines. I met an old friend (Armenian food) again!

Since my son travelled many times to this region, he brought me many recipes and some native ingredients. I become quite interested and further experimented with the help of two Armenian friends. The key challenge was to develop all recipes, so they could be prepared without a *tonir* (traditional fireplace). This cookbook is the result of my year-long efforts, so I deeply appreciate your honest feedback on Amazon.

After quite my unexpected success of five previous cookbooks from the Balkans and the Mediterranean regions, I decided to continue and share even more. I believe that exchanging culture with others is the most beautiful thing in the world. For me, the foods I love and the recipes I like and develop are great ways to pay it forward in life. I hope you like this and other cookbooks that I will publish in the coming months.

At the moment, you can check out my <u>Balkan Cookbook</u>, <u>Greek Cookbook</u>, <u>Serbian Cookbook</u>, <u>Turkish Cookbook</u>, <u>Persian Cookbook</u>, as well as <u>111 recipes for Your Mediterranean Diet</u>.

Once again, I'd be very grateful if you take the time to post a short review on Amazon. Bon appetite!

Respectfully,
Slavka Bodić

Table of Contents

SOUPS 93

Armenian Cuisine

Different cuisines from the Caucasus region have been around for many centuries. However, they changed, developed, and added new elements over time, but remained true to their roots. Many diplomats and travelers say that Armenian and Georgian cuisines are the best in the world. Armenian cuisine is famous for using vegetables, lamb, bread, and many spices. According to scientists, Armenians knew how to bake bread and pioneered the barbeque more than 2500 years ago.

Cattle breeding served as one of the main types of survival in the Armenian highlands. Consequently, the cuisine has been enriched with different types of cheese, Armenian yogurt (*matsun*), and dairy products. Methods and cooking technologies never changed, but the preparation of some meals has adjusted to the modern kitchen environment without losing any traditional taste or authentic quality of the real Armenian cuisine.

In sum, the most popular Armenian traditional product is *lavash* (Armenian bread), which has been included in the list of intangible Cultural Heritage by UNESCO in 2014. Normally, lavash is prepared in a special fireplace called a *tonir*, a tapered cylinder, made of refractory clay and dug in the ground. Apart from *lavash*, this unique baking place is still a key for the traditional preparation of vegetables, soups, smoked chicken, and fish.

Desserts are more delicious than anywhere with *gata* (multi-layered cake) as the queen of all Armenian sweets. Many of them are prepared from fruits, since Armenia is quite a sunny country, but the apricot has always been the ultimate symbol for Armenians. They've been growing it for more than 3000 years and it's still part of many traditional sweets.

The majority of Armenian meals aren't complicated for preparation and that's yet another reason to master this fabulous cuisine.

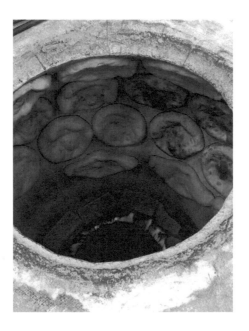

Just In Case

Cooking Measurement Chart

Weight		Measurement				Temperature	
imperial	metric	cup	onces	milliliters	tbsp.	fahrenheit	celsius
1/2 oz	15 g	8 cup	64 oz	1895 ml	128	100 °F	37 °C
1 oz	29 g	6 cup	48 oz	1420 ml	96	150 °F	65 °C
2 oz	57 g	5 cup	40 oz	1180 ml	80	200 °F	93 °C
3 oz	85 g	4 cup	32 oz	960 ml	64	250 °F	121 °C
4 oz	113 g	2 cup	16 oz	480 ml	32	300 °F	150 °C
5 oz	141 g	1 cup	8 oz	240 ml	16	325 °F	160 °C
6 oz	170 g	3/4 cup	6 oz	177 ml	12	350 °F	180 °C
8 oz	227 g	2/3 cup	5 oz	158 ml	11	375 °F	190 °C
10 oz	283 g	1/2 cup	4 oz	118 ml	8	400 °F	200 °C
12 oz	340 g	3/8 cup	3 oz	90 ml	6	425 °F	220 °C
13 oz	369 g	1/3 cup	2.5 oz	79 ml	5.5	450 °F	230 °C
14 oz	397 g	1/4 cup	2 oz	59 ml	4	500 °F	260 °C
15 oz	425 g	1/8 cup	1 oz	30 ml	3	525 °F	274 °C
1 lb	453 g	1/16 cup	1/2 oz	15 ml	1	550 °F	288 °C

Appetizers

Lavash Cheese Sticks

Preparation time: 10 minutes

Cook time: 5 minutes

Nutrition facts: 1 serving 354 kcal (18g protein, 7g fat, 46g carbs)

Ingredients (2 servings)

2 eggs

2 strips of any cheese

2 tablespoon butter

1 teaspoon chopped garlic

1 teaspoon chopped dill

1 piece Armenian lavash

Preparation

Cut the cream cheese into thin strips and beat the eggs well. Chop the garlic and chop the dill finely. Cut the lavash into strips. Then we take a strip of the lavash, put two strips of cheese on it along its length and a little garlic. Next, sprinkle with herbs on top and carefully roll the strip into a roll. Dip the resulting sticks in an egg and fry in butter on both sides until they reach a roasted golden color. It should take 4-6 minutes. Serve to the table with herbs and sour cream.

Lavash Rollups with Mushrooms and Spinach

Preparation time: 20 minutes

Nutrition facts: 1 serving 350 kcal (20g protein, 22g fat, 21g carbs)

Ingredients (4 servings)

20 oz spinach

7 oz mushrooms

7 oz cheese

2 tablespoon mayonnaise

1 teaspoon nutmeg

1 piece of Armenian lavash

Ground black pepper to taste

Salt to taste

Preparation

Cut the spinach 2 to 3 inches above the ground, dry it and chop. Add grated cheese and fried mushrooms, salt, pepper, and nutmeg. Spread the mayonnaise on the lavash, put the filling on it, and roll it up. Leave on for 20 minutes before serving.

Tomatoes With Prosciutto

Preparation time: 10 minutes
Cook time: 15 minutes
Nutrition facts: 1 serving 172 kcal (7.9g protein, 11g fat, 31g carbs)

Ingredients (2 servings)

6 pieces prosciutto
3 cloves garlic
1 piece of chili pepper
1 teaspoon thyme
1 teaspoon rosemary
1 teaspoon balsamic cream
1 teaspoon sugar
1 teaspoon Olive oil
Salt to taste
Ground black pepper to taste
15 oz small tomatoes

Preparation

From 4 layers of foil, form a square container and put the tomatoes in it. Pour the olive oil, and then add sprigs of thyme and rosemary. Cut chili pepper, crush and peel the garlic, and then place them on the bottom of the bowl. Pour the tomatoes with balsamic cream. Sprinkle the tomatoes with sugar, salt, and pepper. Bake the tomatoes in preheated to 360 F in normal mode or with convection for 16 minutes. Cool the tomatoes, put them on a plate, pour the allocated juice, and serve with prosciutto.

Cottage Cheese, Radish and Cucumber in Lavash

Preparation time: 120 minutes

Nutrition facts: 1 serving 250 kcal (14g protein, 4.1g fat)

Ingredients (4 servings)

2 pieces Armenian lavash

3.5 oz. sour cream 20%

8 oz cucumbers

8 oz radish

7 oz. cottage cheese

Preparation

Peel both the cucumbers and radishes. Next, rub on a coarse grater, mix with cottage cheese. Grease the sheets of lavash with sour cream, wrap the filling, and then put in the refrigerator for 60 minutes to soak. Serve.

Ham and Cheese Lavash Pockets

Preparation time: 10 minutes

Cook time: 21 minutes

Nutrition facts: 1 serving 214 kcal (12g protein, 22g fat, 19g carbs)

Ingredients (6 servings)

6 eggs

5.2 oz. cheese

7oz ham

Green onions to taste

1 piece of Armenian lavash

2 cups of water

Preparation

Boil eggs in 2 cups of water for 15 minutes. Grate the cheese on a coarse grater, finely chop the ham, add chopped onions and boiled eggs. Cut each sheet of lavash into 4-6 parts. Wrap the stuffing in them. Fry in a pan on both sides for 3 minutes and then serve.

Vegetable Skewers With Garlic and Basil

Preparation time: 15 minutes

Cook time: 12 minutes

Nutrition facts: 1 serving 132 kcal (3g protein, 7.9g fat, 12g carbs)

Ingredients (6 servings)

0.3 cup olive oil

¼ cup basil leaves

3 cloves garlic

¼ cup white balsamic vinegar

1 teaspoon coarse salt

½ teaspoon freshly ground black pepper

1 onion

1 piece of yellow bell pepper

15 oz finger eggplant

3 pieces zucchini

20 pieces cherry tomatoes

Preparation

Preheat the grill or barbecue. In a bowl, combine the salt, pepper, olive oil, vinegar, chopped basil, and chopped garlic. On skewers, put onion, sliced onion, chopped small pieces of yellow pepper, chopped eggplant, chopped zucchini, and cherry tomatoes and alternate. Pour the marinade. Put the skewers on the grill and fry for 10-12 minutes until cooked, until the vegetables are soft and tender. Serve.

Eggplant Puree With Mixed Vegetables

Preparation time: 20 minutes

Cook time: 60 minutes

Nutrition facts: 1 serving 129 kcal (2.7g protein, 7g fat, 27g carbs)

Ingredients (10 servings)

4 pieces eggplant

7 pieces tomatoes

2 cloves onion

½ cloves garlic

3oz greens

Dried basil to taste

Ground black pepper to taste

½ cup vegetable oil

Preparation

Cut the edges and leaves from small eggplants. Cut them lengthwise into several pieces. Put in a large pot and pour boiling water so that they're immersed. Salt it and leave on for 15 minutes. Drain the water and cut each eggplant into several slices. Pour the oil into a deep-frying pan and heat. Pour the eggplants and, with a little salt, start to brown them thoroughly - almost like potatoes, but avoid overly fried crusts, about 20 minutes.

Close the lid and proceed to peeling the onion. Cut it into large pieces, pour them into another pan. Fry until golden brown and begin to add the tomatoes and onion. Next, peel and chop the garlic and add it to the eggplant. Add pepper and tomatoes, sprinkle with basil, and combine with the eggplant. Then cut the greens and add them into the hot mixture. Let it simmer for another 30 minutes. Serve.

Lavash with Cheese and Crackers

Preparation time: 20 minutes
Cook time: 30 minutes
Nutrition facts: 1 serving 305 kcal (16g protein, 13kcal, 29g carbs)

Ingredients (6 servings)

7 oz chicken fillet

12 pieces of salad leaves

3 pieces of Armenian lavash

5 oz curd cheese

8 1/2 oz sour cream

2 tablespoon mustard

5 cups of water

Ground black pepper to taste

Salt to taste

Crackers to taste

Preparation

Boil the chicken breast in prepared water for 30 minutes. Divide each lavash into two parts, to create six lavash pieces. Stir the sour cream with the mustard and grease the sheets. Spread the lettuce leaves on top, one or two per sheet. On the leaves, add thinly sliced cheese, then a little sour cream mixture. Then put the crackers and diced meat (boiled chicken breast). Wrap the stuffed bread. Keep in the refrigerator for 10 minutes and serve.

Puff Pastries With Leek

Preparation time: 30 minutes
Cook time: 30 minutes
Nutrition facts: 1 serving 322 kcal (8g protein, 11g fat, 39g carbs)

Ingredients (6 servings)

3 pieces of leek

1 puff pastry

1 egg

5 oz. robiola cheese

1 tablespoon olive oil

Pinch of salt

Preparation

In a heated frying pan with olive oil, stew the leek that's cut into rings for 16 minutes under a closed lid. Salt. At the end of cooking, remove the lid for evaporating the liquid. Sprinkle flour on the work surface. Roll the dough into a rectangle as thin as possible. Mash the robiola cheese with a fork into a uniform consistency.

Apply a cheese layer to the dough with a knife, leaving an edge of 1/3 inch free on the long side. Put the leek on top. Beat the egg with salt and brush the free edges of the dough with a brush. Roll the doughs. Place the rolls on a baking sheet covered with paper and spread on top with a beaten egg. Put in an oven preheated to 360 F for 20 minutes. Turn off the oven and open the door. Don't take out the rolls for another 10 minutes and then serve.

Armenian Pickled Grapes

Preparation time: 60 minutes

Cook time: 30 minutes

Nutrition facts: 1 serving: 194 kcal (1g protein, 0.8g fat, 47g carbs)

Ingredients (6 servings)

2 1/2 pound of grapes

1 cup table vinegar

2 oz honey

5 garlic cloves

1 teaspoon cardamom seeds

½ cup water

2/3 oz salt

2 oz sugar

Preparation

Cook marinade from all ingredients (except the grapes) for 30 minutes. Rinse the edges of medium-sized ripe hard grapes. Place the grapes in rows in a sterilized jar. Pour the marinade and leave in a dark, cold place for 70 minutes. Serve.

Rice Pancakes With Arugula, Carrot, Onions, and Meat

Preparation time: 15 minutes
Cook time: 20 minutes
Nutrition facts: 1 serving 195 kcal (9g protein, 14g fat, 32g carbs)

Ingredients (6 servings)

10 rice papers

2 carrots

1 bunch chives

1 pound of lamb or beef

2 green peppers

1 bunch arugula

2 tablespoon salad mix

1 tablespoon soy sauce

2 eggs

Preparation

Marinate the meat in soy sauce, vinegar, and onions. Set it aside for 15 mins. Now take a pan and on the low heat fry the meat for 10-13 minutes. You can alternatively pour the marinade juice on it to make the meat juicier.

Now make an omelet. To do this, mix 2 eggs, a spoonful of sugar, a spoonful of soy sauce and arugula. Fry omelet for 5 minutes and cut it into strip slices. Form a vegetable mixture by cutting the carrots separately in small cubes, while red pepper should be cut into small stripes. Chop green onions and chili pepper. On each prepared sheet of rice paper, spread the greens (salad mixture), then add the meat, on top of it with a strip of omelet and finely the chopped vegetables. Finely, wrap it all together in a pocket form and your pancakes are ready.

Appetizer with Cheese and Matsun

Preparation time: 30 minutes
Cook time: 22 minutes
Nutrition facts: 1 serving 306 kcal (30g protein, 18g fat, 59g carbs)

Ingredients (4 servings)

17 oz cheese

1 oz fresh mint

1 teaspoon salt

1tablespoon garlic

½ teaspoon chili pepper

½ cup milk

1 cup Armenian yogurt (*matsun*)

5 oz sour cream

½ teaspoon ground black pepper

Preparation

Bring the milk to a boil for 18-21 minutes. Cut cheese into slices, then add to milk, and cook for 2 minutes. Put the cheese on a wooden surface and roll it with a rolling pin, like dough. Add finely chopped mint, garlic, pepper, then mix and top with a layer of cheese. Cool in the refrigerator for 16 minutes.

Prepare the sauce by mixing sour cream, Armenian yogurt, and milk. Add finely chopped mint and garlic, along with the rest of the spices. Take the roll from the refrigerator, cut into pieces, and heat. Pour the rolls with sauce. Garnish with pomegranate seeds and fresh mint and serve.

Appetizer With Spinach

Preparation time: 15 minutes

Cook time: 5 minutes

Nutrition facts: 1 serving 225 kcal (8g protein, 16g fat, 52g carbs)

Ingredients (4 servings)

17 oz spinach

7 oz onions

3 oz walnuts

1 green chili pepper

2 cloves of garlic

12 branches cilantro

3 pieces of parsley

Pomegranate kernels to taste

2 tablespoon wine vinegar

Salt to taste

Preparation

Boil the spinach for 5 minutes. Then place in a colander, put on paper towels, and allow it to cool. Finely chop onion, garlic, pepper, cilantro, and parsley. When the spinach has cooled, process it in the meat grinder together with the nuts. Stir everything until smooth, adding wine vinegar and salt. Give it a beautiful shape as balls, put on a plate, and garnish with pomegranate seeds and serve.

Fried Eggplants with Pomegranate Seeds

Preparation time: 15 minutes

Cook time: 10 minutes

Nutrition facts: 1 serving 121 kcal (1.2g protein, 8g fat, 19g carbs)

Ingredients (5 servings)

3 eggplant

1 bunch cilantro

3 cloves of garlic

½ grenade

¼ cup refined oil

Salt to taste

Preparation

Cut the stalk from the eggplant and, without removing the peel, cut into lengthwise slices ¼ inch thick. Heat the pan, pour oil on it, and fry the eggplants for about 5 minutes on each side.

Crush the garlic, cilantro and salt thoroughly in a mortar until you get a smooth consistency. Coat each fried eggplant slice on both sides with paste and put on a dish. Sprinkle the eggplant with pomegranate seeds before serving.

Main Dishes

Beef Heart and Liver Dish (*Tjvjik*)

Preparation time: 5 minutes

Cook time: 30 minutes

Nutrition facts: 1 serving 423 kcal (55.4g protein, 16.3 fat, 13.8g carbs)

Ingredients (4 servings)

1,5 oz coriander

21 oz beef liver

21 oz beef heart

1 big onion

10 oz tomatoes

1 tablespoon basil

2 tablespoon butter

A pinch of salt

A pinch of pepper

Preparation

Cut lengthwise the beef heart and liver. In a saucepan, add butter and put it on the heat. Now add finely sliced onions and stir till they turn golden. Cut the tomatoes into small pieces and add to the mixture of onions. Stir for about 2-3 minutes. Add the heart and liver and lower the fire. Cook for 20-25 minutes. Add the coriander, basil, salt, and pepper. Serve.

Dolma with Beans

Preparation time: 60 minutes

Cook time: 60 minutes

Nutrition facts: 1 serving: 356 kcal (17g protein, 13g fat, 44.2g carbs)

Ingredients

1 teaspoon coriander

¼ cup red beans

¼ cup lentil

1/8 cup cabbage

¼ cup onion

1 tablespoon butter

4 cups water

A pinch of salt

A pinch of black pepper

Preparation

Put beans and lentils into the 1 ½ cups of water for 60 minutes. After that, take them off the water and cook in 2 cups of water for 30 minutes. In a saucepan, add finely diced onions and 1 tablespoon of butter and stir till it turns golden. Add the cooked lentils red beans, salt, and pepper. Stir them for about 4-5 minutes. On the plate put cabbage leaves, add a tablespoon of the cooked mixture, and wrap the leaves. In a pan, add the remaining butter, 1 tablespoon of tomato, and ½ cup of water. Place the wrapped cabbage leaves on it and cook for about 30 minutes before serving.

Rice with Dry Fruits in Pumpkin

Preparation time: 10 minutes
Cook time: 90 minutes
Nutrition facts: 1 serving 304 kcal (6.2g protein, 15g fat, 43g carbs)

Ingredients (8 servings)

4-pound pumpkin
¼ cup almond slices
½ cup basmati rice
½ cup butter
½ cup apples cut in cubes
¼ cup plum dry fruit
¼ cup apricot dry fruit
1 tablespoon honey to taste
Salt to taste

Preparation

Preheat the oven 360 F. In a saucepan, cook the rice in 2 cups of boiling water for about 5 minutes and then leave it aside without the water. Take a pan, add almond, and stir till they turn golden. Add 2 tablespoons of butter, dry fruits, and the cubed apple. Stir for 3 minutes. In a bowl mix the rice and dry fruits mixture. Take the pumpkin, cut the top of it, and remove the seeds. Now fill the pumpkin with the rice and dry fruits mixture, honey, and salt. Finally, cook in the preheated oven for about 90 minutes and then serve.

Stuffed Grape Leaves (*Grape Dolma*)

Preparation time: 30 minutes

Cook time: 60 minutes

Nutrition facts: 1 serving 612 kcal (34g protein, 38g fat, 27g carbs)

Ingredients (6 servings)

1pound minced beef meat

½ cup rice

1 pound of minced pork meat

½ cup minced onion

1 tablespoon coriander

1 tablespoon dry basil

2 tablespoon tomato paste

2 cups water

1 pound of grape leaves

Salt and pepper to taste

Preparation

Start with mincing together the onions, beef, and pork meat. In a big bowl, mix together the rice, minced meat, and onions. Add coriander and dry basil and mix well. Add salt and pepper and leave it aside. Take the grape leaves and put them in a bowl filled with boiling water and leave for 15 minutes.

After the leaves soften, take them off one by one and wrap a tablespoon of the meat mixture into them. Place all dolma in a saucepan and fill with 2 cups of water and 2 tablespoon of tomato paste. Bake on the low heat for about 60 minutes until ready. Serve.

Lamb in Cumin Sauce

Preparation time: 10 minutes

Cook time: 5 minutes

Nutrition facts: 1 serving 192 kcal (41g protein, 13g fat, 1.6g carbs)

Ingredients (6 servings)

2.5 pounds lamb

¼ cup butter

½ teaspoon cumin

1 tablespoon parsley

2 lemons

Salt and pepper to taste

Preparation

In a pan, add butter and cumin and put it on a medium heat. Cut the lamb with thin slices, about ¼ inch. Add salt and pepper to the slices and leave it aside for 5 minutes. Transfer the lamb slices into the pan and stir them continuously for about 2 minutes. Add the lemon juice from two lemons into the remaining cumin mixture in the pan. Finally, add parsley into the pan, stir well, and pour the cumin sauce onto the lamb.

Salmon with Spinach

Preparation time: 25 minutes
Cook time: 15 minutes
Nutrition facts: 1 serving 308 kcal (18g protein, 27g fat, 32g carbs)

Ingredients (4 servings)

8 oz salmon

½ cup spinach

2 tablespoon olive oil

1 cup bulgur

1 cup tomatoes

Soy sauce to taste

Coriander to taste

Salt to taste

Lemon juice to taste

Preparation

Add the bulgur into the bowl and fill with the water. Leave it aside for 20 minutes. Cut the salmon fillet into cubes and add them into the pan filled with 2 tablespoon of olive oil. Put the pan onto medium heat and stir well for about 3 minutes. Add the bulgur, spinach, and soy sauce. Stir for another 3 minutes. Lastly, add the tomatoes coriander and lemon juice and leave it on the heat for about 30 seconds. Serve.

Potato with Milk and Armenian Brandy

Preparation time: 10 minutes

Cook time: 35 minutes

Nutrition facts: 1 serving 317 kcal (7g protein, 23g fat, 32g carbs)

Ingredients (4 servings)

¼ cup brandy

¾ cup butter

2cups milk

4 cups water

1 pound of potato

Parsley to taste

Black pepper to taste

Salt to taste

Preparation

Peel the potatoes and boil them in a saucepan filled with 4 cups of water on medium heat for 15 minutes. Pour off the water and add milk and brandy to the potatoes and cook for another 15-20 minutes. After that, add the butter and diced parsley. Stir them well together and serve.

Minced Beef with Armenian Brandy (*Kufta*)

Preparation time: 15 minutes

Cook time: 50 minutes

Nutrition facts: 1 serving 603 kcal (45.3 g protein, 52g fat, 2g carbs)

Ingredients (5 servings)

2,5 pounds minced beef

½ cup minced onion

1 egg

¼ cup brandy

Preparation

In a bowl, mix the minced beef with onions, egg, and brandy. Mix them so well until you get a smooth consistency. Make balls in the size of your palm. Take a saucepan add 4 cups of water and add the meatballs there. Cook on the medium heat for 45-50 minutes.

Stuffed Chicken with Dry Fruits and Rice

Preparation time: 15 minutes
Cook time: 60 minutes
Nutrition facts: 1 serving 664kcal (44g protein, 51g fat, 38g carbs)

Ingredients (5 servings)

1 whole chicken
¼ cup almond
½ cup dates
¼ cup dried apricots
¼ cup olive oil
1 teaspoon butter
¼ cup raisins
1 teaspoon cinnamon
6 oz basmati rice
Salt and pepper to taste

Preparation

Put all dried fruits together in warm water for 15 minutes. Dry them and set aside. In a small saucepan, add 1 cup of water and the rice. Cook for 10 minutes, then dry it, and set aside. Add olive oil to pan and all the other ingredients, except the chicken. Stir well for 6 minutes. Preheat the oven to 360 F. Take the chicken and stuff it with the rice mixture from the pan. Brush the chicken with prepared butter. Place it onto the baking dish and put in the oven. Cook for 45 minutes and serve.

Spinach with Eggs

Preparation time: 10 minutes

Cook time: 10 minutes

Nutrition facts: 1 serving 125 kcal (8g protein, 8.9g fat, 3g carbs)

Ingredients (4 servings)

1 pound of spinach

2 eggs

1 tablespoon butters

5 green onions stems

2 tablespoon parsley

2 tablespoon cilantro

Salt and pepper to taste

Preparation

Boil the spinach in a cup of water for 5 minutes, then dry it, and set aside. Finely dice all the greenery. Take a pan add butter, spinach, and the diced greenery. Stir for 30 seconds, then break the eggs on them, and stir. Cook for 3 minutes and serve.

Kerusus

Preparation time: 10 minutes

Cook time: 40 minutes

Nutrition facts: 1 serving 616 kcal (28g protein, 34g fat, 45g carbs)

Ingredients (4 servings)

8 potatoes

1 pound of beef

3 onion

3 oz butter

Salt and pepper to taste

Preparation

Peel and slice the potatoes lengthwise and fry them 25 minutes on medium heat, until they are ready. Meanwhile, slice the beef and boil it in 5 cups of water for 25 minutes. Cut the onion in half using moon shaped slices. Take a pan and add the onions and butter there. Stir for 4-5 minutes until they turn golden. Add fried potatoes, beef and golden onions onto each other. Cook for 5 minutes and serve.

Bulgur with Pumpkin

Preparation time: 5 minutes

Cook time: 40 minutes

Nutrition facts: 1 serving 253 kcal (10g protein, 1,2g fat, 43g carbs)

Ingredients (4 servings)

1 cup bulgur

1 onion

1 tablespoon garlic

2 tomatoes

1 tablespoon olive oil

1 pound pumpkin

¼ teaspoon turmeric

Salt a pinch

Pepper a pinch

Preparation

Cut the pumpkin, tomatoes, and onions in cubes and mince the garlic. Add a cup of water and the bulgur in a small saucepan and boil for 11 minutes. In a pan, add garlic and olive oil and stir for 3 minutes. Add pumpkin and onions and stir for another 5 minutes. Afterwards, add the cubed tomatoes into the pan and let it get cooked for 5 more minutes. Finally, add the bulgur there and cook for 15 minutes after stirring. Serve.

Chicken Thighs with Lemon

Preparation time: 5 minutes
Cook time: 30 minutes
Nutrition facts: 1 serving 564 kcal (50g protein, 32g fat, 11g carbs)

Ingredients (4 ingredients)

8 chicken thighs
2 tablespoon olive oil
1 garlic clove
2 tablespoon lemon juice
A pinch of salt and pepper

Preparation

Heat a pan on the medium heat and add a tablespoon lemon juice and the minced garlic clove. Stir for 2 minutes. Take a bowl, put the chicken thighs in it, and add the remaining lemon, salt and pepper. Mix it well. Put the chicken thighs onto the heated pan and lower the heat. Cook for 30 minutes and serve.

Armenian barbeque with Pork (*Khorovats)*

Preparation time: 30 minutes

Cook time: 30 minutes

Nutrition facts: 1 serving 451 kcal (40g protein, 17,4g fat, 22g carbs)

Ingredients (4 servings)

1 onion

2 pounds pork

1 cup of pomegranate juice

7oz tomatoes

1 tablespoon Armenian brandy

2 tablespoon salt

A pinch of pepper

Preparation

Cut the pork in 2-inch pieces. Pour salt and pepper on each piece and place them in a bowl. Cut the onion in half moon slices and add onto the meat. Pour into the bowl the pomegranate juice, brandy, and stir all this mixture together very thoroughly. Place meat into it and get marinated. for about 30 minutes. Cut the tomatoes in slices. Take a skewer and string one after another with the tomato and a piece of meat. Put on the barbeque device for 30 minutes. Serve.

Rice with Pomegranate

Preparation time: 10 minutes
Cook time: 30 minutes
Nutrition facts: 1 serving 657kcal (42g protein, 54g fat, 98g carbs)

Ingredients (4 servings)

2 cups rice

2 pounds beef

½ cup olive oil

1 pomegranate

3 onions

Salt and pepper to taste

Preparation

Squeeze the pomegranate and set it aside. Cut the beef in thin slices, put in the pan, add 5 tablespoon olive oil, and cook on the medium heat for 12 minutes. After 12 minutes add pomegranate juice and diced onions. In meanwhile take a saucepan, add 4 cups of water and 2 cups of rice, the remaining of olive oil and a pinch of salt. Cook the rice for 30 minutes on the medium heat and serve.

Chicken Breast Ragout with Mushrooms and Pepper

Preparation time: 10 minutes
Cook time: 30 minutes
Nutrition facts: 1 serving 438 kcal (46g protein, 22g fat, 21g carbs)

Ingredients (4 servings)

1 red pepper

1 green pepper

2 tomatoes

1 pound of chicken breast

1 cup mushrooms

½ pound tomato sauce

1 onion

½ cup basmati rice

4 tablespoon olive oil

Preparation

Cut into slices the green and red peppers, tomatoes, mushrooms, and the chicken breast. In a pan, add 2 tablespoon of olive oil, sliced green and red peppers, diced tomatoes, and stir them well for 5 minutes. Add the sliced mushrooms and cook for another 3 minutes. Put another pan on the low heat, add a tablespoon of olive oil and pour in the sliced chicken breast.

Cook the chicken for 15-20 minutes; and after that, mix with the green and red pepper combination. Meanwhile, take a saucepan, and cook the rice with a cup of water and olive oil on the medium heat for 20 minutes. Finally, for serving, put the rice and top it with the chicken breast mixture.

Armenian Beef Kebab

Preparation time: 15 minutes
Cook time: 25 minutes
Nutrition facts: 1 serving 374 kcal (30g protein, 33g fat, 13g carbs)

Ingredients (6 servings)

7 oz onion
2 pounds minced beef
10 teaspoon olive oil
5 garlic cloves
Salt and pepper to taste

Preparation
Take a big bowl and add the minced beef. Mince the onion and garlic cloves and add to the beef. Add salt and pepper and mix it well, so that you get a smooth consistency. Take a handful of the mixture and make ellipse-shaped meatballs. Preheat a pan on the medium heat, add there the olive oil. Put the meatballs into the pan and cook for 5 minutes on each side. Total cooking time should be around 22 minutes.

Chicken in Wine with Grapes

Preparation time: 10 minutes
Cook time: 40 minutes
Nutrition facts: 1 serving 582kcal (25g protein, 48g fat, 22g carbs)

Ingredients (5 servings)
4 chicken thighs
3 oz olive oil
½ pound red grapes
8 garlic cloves
½ lemon
1cup white dry wine
Salt and pepper to taste

Preparation
Start with preheating the oven to 350 F. Mince the garlic cloves, add a pinch of salt and pepper, and ½ oz. of olive oil. Now take a bowl, add the chicken thighs there, marinade it with the garlic mixture, and leave it aside for 20 minutes. Take a pan and add the remaining olive oil and start frying the chicken thighs for 20 minutes. Add to the thighs the lemon zest and wine. Cook it for another 10 minutes on medium heat and then add the red grapes. Leave it for another 1 minute before serving.

Stuffed Peppers

Preparation time: 10 minutes

Cook time: 50 minutes

Nutrition facts: 1 serving 325 kcal (17g protein, 12.4g fat, 28g carbs)

Ingredients (6 servings)

20 oz mixed minced meat

16 sweet pepper

3 tomatoes

3 carrots

1 onion

6 oz cheese

1 tablespoon tomato paste

Salt to taste

Dried marjoram and rosemary to taste

Vegetable oil

Preparation

Fry the minced meat in vegetable oil with chopped onions and carrots. Add the finely chopped 5 peppers and 3 tomatoes and a little boiled water. Simmer for 15–20 minutes over low heat. Prepare the remaining peppers for stuffing: remove the legs and the core with seeds and hold for 2-3 minutes in boiling water. Add the salt and the mixture of dried herbs (marjoram, rosemary), and tomato paste to the mixture of minced meat and vegetables. Leave to stew for another 5-7 minutes. Fill the peppers with the prepared mixture and put in a baking dish greased with vegetable oil. Cut the cheese into thin slices and cover with them the stuffed peppers. Bake in the oven at 350 F for 20 minutes. Serve.

Chicken with Pomegranate and Vegetables

Preparation time: 5 minutes

Cook time: 50 minutes

Nutrition facts: 1 serving 484 kcal (22g protein, 67g fat, 72g carbs)

Ingredients (4 servings)

2.5 pounds chicken

1.5 pounds onion

¾ cup vegetable oil

2 tablespoon butter

20 oz pomegranate seeds

Preparation

In a hot frying pan, fry pieces of chicken without oil on both sides for 3-4 minutes, so that the pores of the meat are closed, and it remains juicy. Add vegetable oil to the pan and a large piece of onion cut in half rings. Stew about 40 minutes or until the chicken is fully cooked. Several minutes before the end, add the butter and the pomegranate seeds.

Salmon with Tarragon Leaves

Preparation time: 5 minutes
Cook time: 20 minutes
Nutrition facts: 1 serving 475 kcal (36g protein, 10.2g fat, 27g carbs)

Ingredients (2 servings)
1 salmon
¼ cup water
Sea salt to taste
Tarragon branch to taste

Preparation
Rinse and clean the salmon well. Next, salt, put in a saucepan, pour in a little water, and simmer on low heat for 16 minutes. Remove the saucepan from the fire, carefully transfer the salmon to a dish, cover with a damp cloth and store in a cool place until serving. When serving, garnish the fish with tarragon branches.

Pilaf with Pomegranate, Dried Fruit, and Thyme

Preparation time: 5 minutes

Cook time: 25 minutes

Nutrition facts: 1 serving 361 kcal (11g protein, 24g fat, 48g carbs)

Ingredients (4 servings)

2 tablespoon butter

1 red onion

1 cup basmati rice

2 cups vegetable broth

1 tablespoon shredded fresh thyme

1,5 cup chicken stock

½ cup dried apricots

½ cup ground pistachios

½ cup pomegranate kernels

Salt to taste

Freshly ground black pepper to taste

Preparation

Melt the butter in a saucepan over medium heat. Add the finely chopped onions and fry 5 minutes or until soft. Add the rice and fry for another minute. Pour in the broth and bring to a boil. Close the lid and reduce the heat. Cook for 20 minutes. Remove from the heat and stir with a fork. Stir in the chopped dried fruits, pistachios, pomegranate seeds, and thyme. Add salt, pepper, and serve.

Lamb With Rice

Preparation time: 10 minutes

Cook time: 30 minutes

Nutrition facts: 1 serving 533 kcal (30.2g protein, 41g fat, 47g fat)

Ingredients (4 servings)

1 pound of lamb

2 tablespoon ghee

1 cup rice

Salt and pepper to taste

Preparation

Wash the meat, dry it, and double-pass through a meat grinder. In a deep saucepan, heat half the oil and fry the minced meat until tender 10 minutes. Next, mince the meat. Pour a glass of boiling water, salt and pepper, add rinsed rice, and mix. Cover and cook over low heat for about 20 minutes.

Meatballs with Nuts (*Ishli Kufta*)

Preparation time: 30 minutes
Cook time: 60 minutes
Nutrition facts: 1 serving 662 kcal (31g protein, 72g fat, 41g carbs)

Ingredients (6 servings)
2.5 pounds beef
1 pound of pork
1 cup onions
1 cup walnuts
2 cups ghee
2 cups bulgur
Salt and ground black pepper to taste

Preparation
Prepare the filling by adding pork meat and onions to a meat grinder. Fry the minced meat in a large amount of ghee and add the crushed walnuts. Add salt and pepper to taste. To make the filling for the outer layer, carefully pass the beef through a meat grinder with bulgur twice. From the resulting mass, form balls by making a dimple with your finger, fill it with filling, and give the shape of a "lemon." When done, place it in the freezer. When needed, cook in salted water for 20-25 minutes and serve with lemon.

Armenian Bread with Stuffed Greens

Preparation time: 30 minutes

Cook time: 6 minutes

Nutrition facts: 1 serving 410kcal (12g protein, 4g fat, 64g carbs)

Ingredients (5 servings)

4 cups wheat flour

2 cups water

2 branches scallions

1 tablespoon ghee

1 onion

Salt to taste

Preparation

Knead dough from flour, salt, and cold water, cover, and let it stand for 30 minutes. Cut into pieces and roll thin circles with a diameter of 5 inch. Prepare the filling by removing any hard stems from the greens and chopping the leaves. Cut the onion into very thin half rings and simmer for 4 minutes over medium heat in a saucepan with 1 tablespoon of melted butter until soft.

Remove from the heat and cool. Add the greens to the saucepan and mix. Spread the chopped greens in half a circle of dough, salt, pepper and immediately pinch the edges in the form of a semicircle, trying to prevent the juice from the greens from falling to the edges. Fry in a dry, well-heated frying pan without oil, for 2 minutes on each side and serve hot.

Armenian Ratatouille

Preparation time: 10 minutes

Cook time: 40 minutes

Nutrition facts: 1 serving 85 kcal (2,3g protein, 0.3g fat, 16,2g carbs)

Ingredients (4 servings)

8.5 oz. eggplant

7 oz sweet pepper

8 oz young zucchini

7 oz tomatoes

¼ cup onion

1 teaspoon wine vinegar

7 oz potatoes

1 teaspoon balsamic vinegar

Sea salt and ground black pepper salt to taste

Preparation

Cut all vegetables into flat, round slices with a thickness of no more than ¼ inch. Put the chopped vegetables in a pan with a high side, add the spices, and vinegar. Cook over medium heat with the lid closed for 21–26 minutes. Remove the pan from the stove and put in the oven for 10-15 minutes at medium heat. Serve.

Chicken Legs in Lemon

Preparation time: 5 minutes
Cook time: 30 minutes
Nutrition facts: 1 serving 381kcal (3.2g protein, 27g fat, 40g carbs)

Ingredients (4 servings)

8 chicken legs
2 tablespoon butter
1 garlic clove
2 tablespoon lemon juice
Salt and ground black pepper to taste

Preparation

Melt the butter with chopped garlic and lemon juice over low heat in a pan. Spread salt and pepper over the chicken legs and grease with lemon oil. Preheat the grill or barbecue. Put the legs on the wire rack and fry, constantly turning and greasing with lemon oil, until tender and browned for about 30 minutes. Cool slightly and serve with any sauce.

Johob

Preparation time: 10 minutes
Cook time: 30 minutes
Nutrition facts: 1 serving 616 kcal (18g protein, 42g fat, 82g carbs)

Ingredients (4 servings)

2 pounds onion

3 pounds chicken

7 oz butter

20 oz pomegranate seeds

Seasoning to taste

Preparation

Chop the chicken into small pieces. Melt the butter in a pan and fry the chicken for 16 minutes or until half cooked. Add the onion chopped in half rings and fry for another 15 minutes on low heat. Add the pomegranate seeds and simmer for a while until the grains turn white.

Roasted Lamb Heart

Preparation time: 5 minutes

Cook time: 20 minutes

Nutrition facts: 1 serving 106kcal (12g protein, 2,1g fat, 7g carbs)

Ingredients (2 servings)

8 oz lamb heart

½ cup onions

½ beam cilantro

2 cloves of garlic

Salt to taste

Preparation

Rinse lamb hearts, flatten, remove excess, and divide into pieces 1 ½ x 1 ½ inch. Cut onions lengthwise into four parts and disassemble into petals. In a very hot wok, heat a small amount of vegetable oil and, stirring constantly, to quickly fry the hearts for about 15 minutes. As soon as they're slightly browned, add the onion, chopped garlic and fry, continuously mixing nonstop until the onion becomes slightly transparent, but remains crunchy. Salt to taste and add the chopped cilantro. Remove from the heat and serve.

Traditional Armenian Harissa

Preparation time: 10 minutes
Cook time: 160 minutes
Nutrition facts: 1 serving 548 kcal (11g protein, 27g fat, 57g carbs)

Ingredients (8 servings)

2.5 pounds round grain wheat or Armenian *zavar*

3 pounds chicken

7 oz butter

15 cups water

Salt to taste

Preparation

Sort out the grain wheat and rinse. Put the chicken to boil for 40 minutes and use prepared broth for making harissa. Remove bones from the boiled chicken. Add the pulp to the round grain wheat and chicken broth. Continue to cook for 120 minutes, stirring constantly. At the end of cooking, add butter, salt to taste and boil for another 10 minutes, before serving.

Armenian Pizza (*Lahmajo*)

Preparation time: 60 minutes
Cook time: 10 minutes
Nutrition facts: 1 serving 648 kcal (17g protein, 27g fat, 59g carbs)

Ingredients (6 servings)
2 1/2 pounds of lamb
5 cups wheat flour
½ teaspoon soda
¼ onion
6 cloves garlic
¼ cup yogurt
2 tablespoon tomato paste
Salt and ground red pepper to taste
Parsley to taste

Preparation
Prepare the dough by adding soda to the yogurt. Mix until a foam forms, add salt, gradually add flour, and knead a smooth dough that doesn't stick to your hands. Cover with foil and leave for 45 minutes. In the meantime, put the meat, onions, and garlic through a meat grinder. Next, add the finely chopped herbs, peppers, salt, and tomato paste and then knead a little water. Preheat the oven to 410 F. From the dough, make balls the size of a tennis ball, then roll each piece thinly, transfer to a baking sheet, grease with minced meat and bake for 10 minutes until the bottom of the dough turns pink. Fold the cakes with the meat side to each other.

Beetroot Pasta

Preparation time: 10 minutes
Cook time: 30 minutes
Nutrition facts: 1 serving 218 kcal (7g protein, 3,1g fat, 42g carbs)

Ingredients (4 servings)

8 ½ oz spaghetti

8 oz beetroot

¼ cup dry white wine

1 teaspoon olive oil

1 onion

2 tablespoon nutmeg

2 ½ cup cups water

Preparation

Cut the beetroot into thin strips and chop the onion finely. Fry the beets with strips and then season with salt and pepper to taste before adding wine. Cook spaghetti in salted 2 ½ cups of water for 20 minutes, recline, cool, and fry in oil. To prevent the pasta from sticking to the pan, add some water. Mix the beet strips with spaghetti. Bring to a boil together, then add salt and pepper again. Lastly, sprinkle with nutmeg and serve.

Homemade Armenian Shawarma

Preparation time: 15 minutes

Cook time: 17 minutes

Nutrition facts: 1 serving 621 kcal (12g protein, 48g fat, 60g carbs)

Ingredients (2 servings)

2 pieces of Armenian lavash

7 oz cheese

8 oz ground beef

2 tomatoes

1 bunch green (dill, parsley, basil)

1 onion

2 tablespoon vegetable oil

2 tablespoon butter

2 tablespoon cheese sauce

Salt and ground black pepper to taste

Preparation

Fold the Armenian lavash in half from one edge. Grate the cheese and form half of the available cheese in the shape of a rectangle on a lavash. Fry the minced meat in vegetable oil for 15 minutes. Cut the tomato and lay it on the minced meat. Add sauce or mayonnaise on it. Cut onions into thin half rings and spread them over the sauce.

Finely chop the greens and sprinkle over the onion. Season with salt and pepper to taste. Wrap the edges of the lavash. Roll the first roll and repeat the process with the second. Heat a frying pan with butter, put shawarma in it and fry on both sides over medium heat until a crispy golden crust form. Frying should be about 2 minutes per edge. Serve when finished.

Shrimp Ravioli with Foie Gras in Shrimp Sauce

Preparation time: 15 minutes
Cook time: 40 minutes
Nutrition facts: 1 serving 671 kcal (38g protein, 51g fat, 83g carbs)

Ingredients (4 servings)

1 cup tiger prawns

3 tablespoon foie gras

1 lemon

¼ cup of shrimp, keep the shells

½ carrot

½ onion

1 cup water

2 tablespoon cream 10%

1 teaspoon cognac

1 teaspoon tomato paste

1 teaspoon vegetable oil

1 cup wheat flour

1 egg yolk

2 teaspoon olive oil

1 pinch salt

1 pinch ground black pepper

Preparation

Mix well the flour, egg yolk, olive oil, and water in order to make dough. Set it aside. In a saucepan, add finely chopped carrots, tomato paste, chopped onions, vegetable oil, and the shrimp shells. After 2 minutes, add a cup of water and cook for another 15 minutes on low heat. Filter the liquid through a sieve. Take a pan and put on the low heat, add the shrimps and tiger prawns and the sieved broth, cream, a teaspoon of olive oil, foie gras, and salt. Cook no more than a minute and beat this with a blender. Put the blended mixture on the heat again and add cognac, all the other herbs, and boil on the low heat for 7-10 minutes. Cut squares from the dough, add a tablespoon of shrimp mixture, and fold them. Boil for 8-10 minutes and serve.

Breakfast

Feta Cheese Omelet

Preparation time: 5 minutes

Cook time: 10 minutes

Nutrition facts: 1 serving: 231 kcal (8g protein, 11.1g fat, 62g carbs)

Ingredients

1 cup milk

2 leaves of green salad

3 oz. *bryndza* cheese (feta or other white cheese is good, too)

1 teaspoon butter

4 eggs

Pinch of salt

Ground black pepper to taste

Preparation

Beat eggs, add to the milk, and whisk well. Cut the salad and *bryndza* cheese into small pieces and mix everything. Melt a small piece of butter in a pan. Pour the egg mixture into the pan. Close the lid and cook over moderate heat for 5–7 minutes. Sprinkle salt and pepper one minute before cooking. Use a spatula to wrap the omelet. Serve warm.

Traditional Armenian Sandwich

Preparation time: 30 minutes
Cook time: 18 minutes
Nutrition facts: 1 serving 319kcal (21g protein, 4,9g fat, 21g carbs)

Ingredients (3 servings)

16 oz chicken fillet

1 eggplant

2 potatoes

2 tomatoes

3 tablespoon *adjika*

2 tablespoon zucchini caviar

1 bunch parsley

1 bunch dill

2 cloves of garlic

Salt to taste

Paprika to taste

6 pieces of pita bread

Preparation

Rinse the chicken fillet and divide into three parts. Add salt and pepper. Set aside for 15 minutes; in the meantime, begin cooking the sauce.

Mix in equal proportions of adjika and squash caviar. Stir thoroughly until smooth. Add two squeezed garlic cloves. Cook the ingredients parallel, but separately. Deep-fry the chicken, eggplant, and potatoes. Cut the potatoes and zucchini into slices and add salt and red pepper before placing into fried oil.

After the eggplant is ready, send it to a bowl with chopped greens and garlic. Finely chop the chicken fillet and lay out the pita bread. Add the sauce and sprinkle with herbs. Add the fried eggplant and potatoes. Add the chopped tomato slices. Wrap the pita bread and fry on both sides. Serve warm.

Lavash with Cheese and Egg

Preparation time: 5 minutes

Cook time: 9 minutes

Nutrition facts: 1 serving 655 kcal, (19g protein, 27g fat, 85g carbs)

Ingredients (4 servings)

2 pieces of Armenian lavash

2 tablespoon cheese

1 egg

1 tablespoon butter

5 cups water

Salt to taste

Preparation

Preheat the pan and fry the butter in it. Dip 2 lavashes in salted water and put them in a pan. Fry on both sides for 2 minutes. Add 1-2 tablespoons of salted water to make the lavash leaves soft. Break the egg into the center of the lavash bread and spread it over the entire surface. Fry a little for 4 minutes. When the egg sets on the bread, add the grated cheese. For a few seconds, fry the cheese side of our dish and fold the lavash bread in half (cheese and egg side inward). Serve warm.

Millet Porridge with Pumpkin

Preparation time: 15 minutes

Cook time: 30 minutes

Nutrition facts: 1 serving 337 kcal (7g protein, 11g fat, 58g carbs)

Ingredients (4 servings)

1 cup wheat germs

4 cups milk

1 cup water

½ pound grated pumpkin

1 tablespoon butter

4 tablespoon sugar

½ teaspoon salt

Ground cinnamon on the tip of a knife

Preparation

Cut pumpkin into 2 parts, free from seeds, and peeled. Put one half in the refrigerator. Rinse millet under cold water. Add grated pumpkin, butter, sugar, salt, millet, milk, water in the bowl of a multicooker. Set the "milk porridge" mode for 20 minutes and then simmer the porridge for another 13 minutes under the closed lid. Open, mix, serve in portions, and add cinnamon.

Armenian Pumpkin Porridge

Preparation time: 10 minutes

Cook time: 30 minutes

Nutrition facts: 1 serving 361 kcal (6,4g protein, 22g fat, 38g carbs)

Ingredients (4 servings)

1 ½ pound pumpkin

1 ½ cups milk

½ cup rice

4 tablespoon ghee

1 tablespoon sugar

1 cup water

Pinch of salt

Preparation

Peel the pumpkin, remove the seeds, chop, place in a saucepan, and pour with warmed milk. Cook a rice in 1 cup of water for 15 minutes. Add the half-cooked rice to the pumpkin with melted butter, sugar, salt, and mix well. Cover the pan with a lid, cook porridge for 16 minutes or until the pumpkin is ready. Serve warm.

Salads

Armenian Red Bean Salad

Preparation time: 10 minutes

Nutrition facts: 4 servings: 105 kcal (5g protein, 3.2g fat, 10.7g carbs)

Ingredients

1 bunch fresh cilantro

2 cloves of garlic

1 bunch parsley

1 tablespoon olive oil

1 teaspoon lemon juice

1 stalk red basil

1 cup boiled red beans

Preparation

Grind the cilantro and parsley and then tear the basil with your hands. Mix with the beans. Crush the garlic in a garlic squeezer or chop with a knife and add to the salad and mix. Squeeze the juice from the lemon and pour into the salad. Season the dish with olive oil and stir well before serving.

Yerevan Mushroom Salad

Preparation time: 10 minutes

Cook time: 5 minutes

Nutrition facts: 1 serving 136 kcal (5g protein, 7g fat, 12g carbs)

Ingredients (4 servings)

8 oz mushroom

8 ½ oz sweet pepper

¼ cup bacon

½ cup celery root

4 tablespoon chopped parsley

1 tablespoon vegetable oil

Salt and ground black pepper to taste

Preparation

Cut the bacon into small cubes and the mushrooms into slices. Put a pan onto the fire with 2 tablespoon of olive oil. After 2 minutes, reduce the fire, add the mushrooms, and fry them for another 3 minutes. Sprinkle the mushrooms with herbs, mix, remove from heat and cool. Chop the pepper and celery into strips, combine, season with oil, salt, pepper, and mix well. Place the vegetables on the dish and lay the fried mushrooms on top.

Salad with Carrots and Cheese

Preparation time: 15 minutes

Nutrition facts: 1 serving 148 kcal (1.2g protein, 12g fat, 8.7g carbs)

Ingredients (4 servings)

¼ cup cheese

3 tablespoon mayonnaise

1 carrot

1 garlic clove

Preparation

Grate carrots and cheese. Squeeze the garlic into the salad and season with mayonnaise. Mix and serve.

Armenian Vegetable Salad

Preparation time: 20 minutes
Nutrition facts: 1 serving 64 kcal (5.4g protein, 0.5g fat, 17g carbs)

Ingredients (4 servings)

6 tomatoes
5 cucumbers
3 sweet pepper
3 cloves of onion
1 bunch cilantro
1 bunch basil
1 bunch parsley
1 teaspoon vinegar (3%)
Salt and ground black pepper to taste

Preparation

Wash and peel the cucumbers and tomatoes. Wash the bell pepper and cut the middle with seeds and a tail. Cut everything into thin circles. Peel and chop the onion into thin rings. Rinse and chop finely. Put the vegetables in a deep salad bowl in layers, lightly salt and pepper each layer, and then add the onion on top. Pour vinegar, sprinkle with herbs, and let it brew for 14 minutes before serving.

Summer Salad with Linseed Oil

Preparation time: 20 minutes

Nutrition facts: 1 serving 221 kcal (2g protein, 8.4g fat, 17g carbs)

Ingredients (4 servings)

1 bunch fresh cilantro

2 tomatoes

4 cucumbers

½ beam dill

1 bunch radish

2 tablespoon flaxseed oil

2 tablespoon sunflower unrefined oil

1.5 tablespoon flax seeds

Salt and pepper to taste

Preparation

Cut cucumbers lengthwise into halves, and then very thin slices. If the cucumbers aren't large, you can just form circles. Wash the radish well, remove the tops, and cut into very thin circles, too. Cut the tomatoes into large slices. Finely chop the greens by removing the stiff ends of the stems. Season with linseed oil and unrefined sunflower and flaxseed oil. Add a spoonful of flax seeds and mix well. Salt to taste and decorate on top with the remaining 1/2 tablespoons of flax seeds.

Cabbage Salad with Arugula and Soy Sauce

Preparation time: 10 minutes
Nutrition facts: 1 serving 351 kcal (17g protein, 6g fat, 36g carbs)

Ingredients (2 servings)

8 oz white cabbage
1 bunch arugula
2 tablespoon soy sauce
1 green bell pepper
2 tablespoon white sesame seeds
1 lemon
1 tablespoon vegetable oil
1 cucumber

Preparation

Chop the cabbage and cucumber into squares, chop the pepper into strips, and cut the bunch of arugulas in half. Put all vegetables in a salad bowl and mix well. Squeeze lemon juice into the salad, add soy sauce, oil, and pour sesame seeds. Mix and serve.

Armenian Red Bean Salad with Raisins

Preparation time: 10 minutes

Cook time: 60 minutes

Nutrition facts: 1 serving 174 kcal (6.2g protein, 7g fat, 19g carbs)

Ingredients (4 servings)

2 onion

8 oz red beans

2 tablespoon vinegar

¼ cup vegetable oil

1 bunch greens

2 cloves of garlic

1 tablespoon raisins

Salt and ground black pepper to taste

Preparation

Sort red beans, rinse, boil in the water for 60 minutes or until cooked. Dry the beans, sprinkle with salt, pepper, and chopped herbs. For dressing, mix the vinegar with vegetable oil. Add chopped garlic and raisins. Cut the onions into thin rings and sprinkle on the salad.

Armenian Tabbouleh

Preparation time: 60 minutes
Nutrition facts: 1 serving 219 kcal (4g protein, 12g fat, 21g carbs)

Ingredients (5 servings)
1 bunch fresh cilantro
7 oz bulgur
3 tomatoes
1 onion
4tablespoon vegetable oil
1 stalk parsley
2 cups water
Salt and ground black pepper to taste

Preparation
Place bulgur in a bowl and fill it with 2 cups of boiling water. Soak for 30 minutes, drain, shake. In a bowl, mix the prepared bulgur, tomato, parsley, cilantro, salt, and vegetable oil. Stir and refrigerate for at least 30 mins before serving. Stir everything before serving.

Salad With Omelet and Shrimps

Preparation time: 5 minutes

Cook time: 5 minutes

Nutrition facts: 1 serving 210 kcal (21g protein, 12g fat, 6.7g carbs)

Ingredients (4 servings)

8 oz peeled shrimps

1 bunch chives

7 oz. iceberg lettuce

2 eggs

7 radishes

1 tablespoon cream cheese

3 tablespoon grated cheese

1 teaspoon butter

3 tablespoon mayonnaise

1 tablespoon of 20% sour cream

Salt and ground black pepper to taste

Preparation

Boil the shrimps, hold them in boiling water for 1 minute, rinse with cold water, and drop them into a sieve. Tear the lettuce leaves, then chop the radishes, and green onions. Put the shrimp, onion, and radish in a salad bowl. Cook the omelet by mixing the eggs, grated cheese, and cream cheese. Fry the omelet in butter on both sides for 4 minutes. Cool it and cut into small cubes or strips. Add to the salad.

For the dressing, the mix mayonnaise with sour cream, salt and pepper to taste, and pour into a salad and mix.

Armenian Spring Salad

Preparation time: 10 minutes
Nutrition facts: 1 serving 150 kcal (4g protein, 2g fat, 26g carbs)

Ingredients (2 servings)

1 green apple

2 cucumbers

½ tablespoon sunflower oil

1 garlic clove

4 green onion sprigs

4 stalks dill

Lemon juice to taste

Wine vinegar to taste

Preparation

Grate a large apple on a coarse grater. Remove the peel from the cucumbers and grate, too. Chop the garlic, onions, and dill (without stalks, only leaves). Mix with apples and cucumbers. Sprinkle with vinegar, lemon juice, and oil and mix before serving.

Eggplant Salad

Preparation time: 15 minutes
Cook time: 15 minutes
Nutrition facts: 1 serving 120 kcal (4g protein, 0,2g fat, 21g carbs)

Ingredients (4 servings)
4 eggplants

1 white onion

4 tomatoes

9 garlic cloves

1 tablespoon sugar

Dill to taste

Parsley to taste

Salt to taste

Ground black pepper to taste

Vegetable oil to taste

Preparation
Cut the eggplants into cubes, salt, and set aside. After 30 minutes, rinse under running water. Peel and finely chop the onion. Pour a small amount of vegetable oil into the pan, add the onion, sprinkle it with sugar, and fry for 6 minutes or until light golden brown. Add the eggplant and simmer under the lid over low heat until cooked, about 10 more minutes. Put the stewed eggplant with onions in a salad bowl, add diced tomatoes, chopped herbs, chopped garlic, salt, and vinegar. Mix well, cool and serve.

Tomato Salad with Adjika

Preparation time: 15 minutes

Nutrition facts: 1 serving 219 kcal (4g protein, 12g fat, 21g carbs)

Ingredients (2 servings)

½ pound tomatoes

3 tablespoon sour cream

1 bunch green basil

1 tablespoon dried cilantro

½ teaspoon dry adjika

Any white cheese to taste

Salt to taste

Preparation

Peel and chop the tomatoes and add cheese. Mix sour cream, cilantro, and finely chopped basil to taste. Season the tomatoes with sauce. The salad can be decorated with a spring of basil.

Vegetable Salad With Walnuts

Preparation time: 15 minutes

Nutrition facts: 1 serving 349 kcal (10g protein, 21g fat, 29g carbs)

Ingredients (2 servings)

7 oz tomatoes

7 oz cucumbers

1 tablespoon parsley

1 teaspoon red basil

½ small red onion

2 teaspoon green peppers

1 teaspoon white wine vinegar

1 teaspoon sunflower oil

¼ cup walnuts

1 pinch *khmeli suneli* (or similar spice)

1 pinch saffron

Preparation

Slice each ingredient, season, and mix. Add salt to taste and serve.

Green Salad

Preparation time: 10 minutes
Nutrition facts: 1 serving: 78 kcal (2g protein, 0,2g fat, 7g carbs)

Ingredients (2 servings)

½ cucumbers

1 teaspoon chives

½ cup pink tomatoes

2 tablespoon pomegranate sauce

1 teaspoon any spice mix

5 mint leaves

5 tarragon leaves

3 parsley leaves

1 tablespoon dill

1 teaspoon cilantro

Preparation

Process, rinse, and dry the leaves of greens. Add the sliced tomatoes to them. Put in a plate, sprinkle with the pomegranate and spice mixture. Finally, pour with pomegranate sauce.

Boiled Beetroot Salad With Walnuts And Spices

Preparation time: 15 minutes

Cook time: 40 minutes

Nutrition facts: 1 serving 261 kcal (8g protein, 2g fat, 17g carbs)

Ingredients (7 servings)

2 bunches fresh cilantro

1 1/2 cups walnuts

1 red onion

4 cloves of garlic

2 teaspoons saffron

2 tablespoon vinegar

2 ½ pounds of beetroot

2 teaspoon coriander seeds

3 cups of water

Salt and ground red pepper to taste

Preparation

Cut the onion into thin half rings. Grind the nuts. Mash the garlic to a state of paste. Grind the greens. Combine all the ingredients, season with spices, add vinegar, and mix until smooth. Wash the beets and boil for 45 minutes in 3 cups of water. Peel the cooked beets and cut them into short, thin strips. Mix with dressing.

Warm Salad with Chicken and Almonds

Preparation time: 80 minutes

Cook time: 20 minutes

Nutrition facts: 1 serving 631 kcal (11g protein, 29g fat, 78g carbs)

Ingredients (2 servings)

6 oz chicken fillet

1 tablespoon adjika

½ cucumber

10 leaves of lettuce salad

1 teaspoon olive oil

1 teaspoon lemon juice

1 teaspoon chives

½ cup walnut sauce

1 teaspoon garlic

½ teaspoon vinegar

1 pinch dried cilantro

½ teaspoon saffron

1 teaspoon red curry paste

1 tablespoon tom yam paste

3 tablespoon almonds

2 tablespoon water

Preparation

Chop the green onions. Marinate the chicken in red adjika, dilute with olive oil, and lemon juice. Add the green onions and almonds and leave for 60 minutes. Chop the garlic, add vinegar, saffron, red curry paste, tom-yam paste, almonds and water to make the dressing. Grill chicken fillet for 22 minutes or until cooked. Cut the cucumber and lettuce and place them on a plate together with chicken. Pour the salad with the prepared dressing and decorate with almond petals. Serve warm.

Pear and Pickle Salad

Preparation time: 10 minutes

Nutrition facts: 1 serving 182 kcal (2g protein, 3.7g fat, 19.1g carbs)

Ingredients (4 servings)

4 pears

12 walnuts

1 pickle

3 tablespoon kefir or sour cream

Preparation

Cut the pears into two and pull out the core with a spoon. Peel the walnuts. Insert the kernels of walnuts into the pears, pour over kefir or sour cream, and sprinkle with finely chopped pickles.

Tomato and Egg Salad with Peanut Sauce

Preparation time: 15 minutes
Cook time: 10 minutes
Nutrition facts: 1 serving 323 kcal (9g protein, 26g fat, 18g carbs)

Ingredients (4 servings)

15 oz tomatoes

1 onion

3 egg

¾ cup walnuts

1 garlic clove

1 cilantro

2 stalks parsley

1 teaspoon dill

5 teaspoon water

Vinegar to taste

Red peppers to taste

Salt to taste

Preparation

Process the nuts, cilantro, pepper, garlic and onions in a blender. Pour a 5 teaspoon of water into the resulting mass, after adding a few drops of vinegar to it. Boil the eggs for 10 minutes. Place the sliced tomatoes and circles of hard-boiled eggs in layers on a plate. Pour the sauce and sprinkle with dill and parsley.

Cucumber Salad with Armenian Yogurt

Preparation time: 10 minutes
Cook time: 25 minutes
Nutrition facts: 1 serving 297 kcal (11g protein, 19g fat, 31g carbs)

Ingredients (4 servings)

2 cups yogurt (*Matsun*)
4 cucumbers
2 chicken breasts
4 cups of water
1 cup prunes
4 tablespoon walnuts

Preparation

Boil the chicken breast about 25 minutes or until tender. Next, cool and cut into small cubes. Dice the cucumbers. Cut prunes into 4 parts per piece. Lightly chop the peeled walnut. Mix all ingredients, season with yogurt, salt to taste, and serve.

Soups

Armenian Soup (*Kololak*)

Preparation time: 10 minutes

Cook time: 80 minutes

Nutrition facts: 1 serving 221 kcal (12g protein, 10.2 fat, 28.9g carbs)

Ingredients (6 servings)

10 oz boneless beef

2 tablespoon rice

2 tablespoon wheat germs

1 onion

2 potato

1 egg

1 teaspoon vegetable oil

1 teaspoon tomato paste

2 bay leaf

1 bunch parsley

5 unprocessed black pepper peas

7 cups of water

Salt to taste

Paprika to taste

Preparation

Wash the beef, separate the flesh from the bones. Put the bones in the pan, pour water, and cook for 60 mins. Peel the onion, finely chop it and fry in warmed oil for 5 minutes. Mix half the onion, wheat germs with rice and chopped parsley. Add salt and pepper to taste. Pass the meat through a meat grinder, combine with the rice mixture, eggs, salt, and pepper. Knead thoroughly until smooth. Form half-palm, flat cakes of minced meat. Bind the edges to make a ball. Now bring the broth to a boil. Peel the potatoes and cut into large pieces. Add the potatoes, the remaining onion, bay leaf, and pepper peas, slightly mashed in a mortar, cook for 10 minutes. Put tomato paste in the broth, mix well. Add meatballs to the soup and cook for 15 minutes before serving.

Quick Soup with Turkey and Brown Rice

Preparation time: 5 minutes

Cook time: 30 minutes

Nutrition facts: 1 serving 351 kcal (22g protein, 16g fat, 57g carbs)

Ingredients (6 servings)

½ pound onions

6 1/2 cup chicken stock

1 garlic clove

8 oz carrots

2 turkey escalope

10 oz tomatoes in own juice

1.5 cups brown basmati rice

3 tablespoon minced parsley

Preparation

Boil rice in boiling water until cooked and then drain. In a large saucepan, heat ¼ cups of chicken stock over medium heat. Add finely chopped onions and carrots and cook for about 6 minutes or until the carrots are soft. Add chopped garlic and cook another minute. Add the remaining broth, chopped tomatoes, diced turkey, and rice. Cook for 20 minutes and sprinkle with parsley and serve.

Armenian Lamb and Tarragon Soup

Preparation time: 10 minutes
Cook time: 110 minutes
Nutrition facts: 1 serving 468 kcal (27g protein, 12g fat, 59g carbs)

Ingredients (7 servings)

8 cups water

2 ½ pounds lamb on the bone

1 onion

8 potato

1 bunch fresh tarragon

3 bay leaf

5 peas allspice

Vegetable oil to taste

Preparation

Pour cold water into the pan, add the lamb in it, and boil. Remove the foam and cook the lamb broth for about 85-95 minutes. Strain it through gauze to maintain the transparency of the broth. Remove the meat, cut into small pieces, and return to the broth. Bring to a boil and then add diced potatoes into the soup.

Add vegetables and spices. After 10 minutes or when the potatoes are cooked, add onions that are fried in vegetable oil (sliced in half rings), tarragon twigs, pepper, and bay leaf. Add salt to taste and cook another 10 minutes. Serve the soup hot, after removing the tarragon sprigs from it.

Soup with Rice and Eggs

Preparation time: 10 minutes
Cook time: 30 minutes
Nutrition facts: 1 serving 85 kcal (4g protein, 2g fat, 17g carbs)

Ingredients (6 servings)
4 tablespoon rice
8 cups vegetable broth
2 egg
1 cup water
1 tablespoon parsley
Salt to taste

Preparation

Cook 1 egg until hard-boiled. Pour the broth into a saucepan and bring to a boil for about 10 minutes. Add rice, let the soup boil again, and simmer it for 15 minutes to cook the rice. When done, crush the other egg into the soup, salt it, sprinkle with finely chopped parsley and hard-boiled egg. Serve immediately.

Ham and Bean Soup

Preparation time: 75 minutes

Cook time: 40 minutes

Nutrition facts: 1 serving 495 kcal (21g protein, 19g fat, 81g carbs)

Ingredients (5 servings)

6 cloves garlic

10 cups meat broth

1 onion

1 sweet pepper

3 tablespoon olive oil

1 teaspoon ground paprika

1 tomato

1 ½ cup sausages

½ cup smoked brisket

¼ pound ham

2 bay leaf

Salt to taste

Ground black pepper to taste

5 tablespoon chopped parsley

1 cup white beans

A pinch dried thyme

Preparation

Sort and rinse beans. Next, soak in cold water for 60 minutes. Bring it to a boil. Peel 2 cloves of garlic, add to the pan with thyme, cook under the lid for about 60 minutes. Drain the water. Pour the meat broth and oil into the pan and bring it to the heat. Peel the onion and chop the remaining garlic finely. Fry for 2-3 minutes, add paprika.

Wash the tomato, cut into small cubes, add to the pan. Simmer for 6 minutes. Finely chop the sausages, brisket, and ham. Put in a pan, add bay leaf. Cook under a lid over low heat for about 20 minutes. At the end of cooking, remove the bay leaf. Add half of the parsley, remove from heat, let stand 20 minutes. Serve sprinkled with remaining herbs.

Healthy Soup with Cherry Tomatoes and Dill

Preparation time: 5 minutes

Cook time: 60 minutes

Nutrition facts: 1 serving 78 kcal (1.7 protein, 0.1g fat, 7g carbs)

Ingredients (7 servings)

5 cups water

2 onion

2 carrot

1 teaspoon sea salt

7 oz zucchini

8 oz cherry tomatoes

1 bunch dill

4 garlic cloves

Preparation

Wash and peel the carrots, cut into circles, and dip in boiling water. Dip the garlic into the pan without chopping. Cut the onion into rings and add to the pan. Onions and carrots should cook for about 30 minutes. Add salt. Cut the zucchini into thin slices and add to the soup. Next, cook another 10 minutes. Cut the cherry into 4 parts, add to the pan and cook for 15 minutes. Finally, add the finely chopped dill and cook for 2 minutes before serving.

Soup Puree with Basil and Pumpkin

Preparation time: 10 minutes

Cook time: 25 minutes

Nutrition facts: 6 servings: 116 kcal (5g protein, 1g fat, 31g carbs)

Ingredients

5 pounds pumpkin

1 onion

1 tomato

2 stalks celery stalk

Parsley to taste

Basil to taste

3 garlic cloves

Ground chili to taste

Ground black pepper to taste

Olive oil to taste

Peeled roasted pumpkin seeds to taste

1 cup water

Preparation

Peel the pumpkin, remove seeds, cut into large pieces. Cut celery, onions, a little hot pepper and fry in oil. Add pumpkin, tomato, a cup of boiling water and simmer for 20 minutes. Salt, pepper, grind with a blender. Serve with greens and pumpkin seeds.

Lentil Soup With Spinach

Preparation time: 5 minutes

Cook time: 40 minutes

Nutrition facts: 4 servings: 255 kcal (6g protein, 8.2g fat, 17.2g carbs)

Ingredients

1 pound of lentils

6 cups water

7 oz spinach

4 oz ghee

5 oz onions

7 oz green pepper

1 tablespoon cilantro

Preparation

Cook lentils in water for about 20 minutes or until half cooked. Then add onion and bell pepper, chopped into strips, into lentils. Cook for another 20 minutes and 2 minutes before serving, add chopped fresh spinach, and cilantro to the soup. Add salt and pepper to taste.

Armenian Matsun Soup

Preparation time: 5 minutes

Cook time: 35 minutes

Nutrition facts: 1 serving 422 kcal (16g protein, 11g fat, 69g carbs)

Ingredients (6 servings)

2 tablespoon fresh cilantro

21 oz Armenian yogurt (*Matsun*)

15 oz round grain wheat (*Zavar*)

1 tablespoon butter

3 tablespoon wheat flour

¼ cup onion

1 egg

½ cup sour cream

2 cups water

Preparation

Mix beaten *matsun*, flour, and a beaten egg. Stir well, add water and put on a low fire. Mix constantly with a wooden spoon or spatula and don't allow it to boil. Boil the *zavar* separately for about 20 minutes and then add it to the *matsun*. Continue to cook for 10 more minutes. Fry the onion in butter until soft, add it to the soup, and stir. Salt and then add finely chopped cilantro and sour cream. Serve warm.

Armenian Lamb and Rice Soup

Preparation time: 5 minutes

Cook time: 80 minutes

Nutrition facts: 1 serving 440 kcal (23g protein, 37g fat, 60g carbs)

Ingredients (4 servings)

1 pound of lamb brisket

½ cup rice

1 onion

1 cup plums

2 tablespoon ghee

1 bunch parsley

Salt and ground black pepper to taste

Preparation

Cut the lamb brisket into small pieces, about 2 oz each. Add water and periodically remove the foam. Next, cook the lamb until cooked for about 60 mins. Remove the meat and strain the broth. Put the cooked meat in a pan, pour it with hot strained broth, add rice, washed yellow plum, finely chopped and fried onions, pepper, salt, and cook for 19 minutes or until rice is cooked. Sprinkle with parsley when serving.

Okra Soup

Preparation time: 10 minutes

Cook time: 60 minutes

Nutrition facts: 1 serving 504 kcal (21g protein, 49g fat, 98g carbs)

Ingredients (4 servings)

2 1/2 pounds of beef

20 oz okra

7 oz tomatoes

4 oz onions

½ cup butter

¼ cup greens

Salt and ground black pepper to taste

Preparation

Boil the beef brisket for 35-45 minutes or until cooked. Strain the broth. While the meat is being cooked, melt the butter in a separate saucepan, add onion, bell pepper, peeled tomatoes, and fresh okra. Simmer all the ingredients together for 19-22 minutes. Then add cooked meat to vegetables and pour in strained broth, salt, pepper, and bay leaf and bring to a boil. Boil for 6-7 minutes. Add coarsely chopped cilantro, dill and serve.

Watermelon Soup

Preparation time: 15 minutes

Nutrition facts: 1 serving 152 kcal (4g protein, 2g fat, 31g carbs)

Ingredients (4 servings)

8 cups watermelon pulp

1 cucumber

½ red bell pepper

¼ cup shredded basil leaves

¼ cup chopped parsley

3 tablespoon red wine vinegar

1 shallot onion

2 tablespoon extra-virgin olive oil

Salt to taste

Preparation

In a large bowl, mix the diced watermelon pulp, the peeled and diced cucumber, the diced pepper, basil, parsley, vinegar, chopped shallot, and olive oil. Grind the mixture in a blender and pour into a bowl to the remaining ingredients. Salt to taste and serve.

Traditional Veal Soup (*Khashlama*)

Preparation time: 5 minutes

Cook time: 60 minutes

Nutrition facts: 1 serving 300 kcal (29g protein, 6g fat, 71g carbs)

Ingredients (8 servings)

2 1/2 pounds veal

1 parsley root

1 celery root

½ clove garlic

2 tablespoon chopped parsley

Salt to taste

Preparation

Cut the veal in small pieces. Then pour water, so that it covers the meat. Before boiling, remove the foam, add the roots of parsley and celery, and remove them at the end of cooking. It should take about 60 mins to become fully cooked. About 5 minutes before the meat is ready, add salt to the soup. Before serving, put crushed garlic, a piece of meat, finely chopped parsley on each plate, and a small amount of meat broth.

Armenian Borsch

Preparation time: 10 minutes

Cook time: 60 minutes

Nutrition facts: 1 serving 201 kcal (5g protein, 10g fat, 23g carbs)

Ingredients (8 servings)

2 1/2 pounds white cabbage

2 carrots

1 beetroot

4 potatoes

2 sweet pepper

2 bay leaf

1 1/2 tablespoon tomato paste

½ cup butter

1 onion

Parsley to taste

Dill to taste

Basil to taste

Cilantro to taste

Paprika to taste

Ground black pepper to taste

Preparation

Put butter in a pan and fry finely chopped onions, adding tomato paste, 1 cup of water, paprika, and black pepper. Add finely chopped potatoes, cabbage, bell peppers, carrots, and beets, chopped in a blender. Fill with water so that it covers the vegetables. Add chopped greens, bay leaves, and salt to taste. Cook over low heat under the lid for 55-60 minutes after boiling and then serve.

Traditional Armenian Cold Soup (*Matsnabrdosh*)

Preparation time: 30 minutes
Nutrition facts: 1 serving 267 kcal (12g protein, 17.2g fat, 39g carbs)

Ingredients (2 servings)

21 oz Armenian yogurt (*matsun*)
1 bunch basil
1 bunch dill
1 bunch cilantro
2 cucumbers
Pinch of salt
2 teaspoon walnuts

Preparation

Wash and peel the cucumbers and cut into small cubes. Finely chop the greens. Beat the *matsun* either with a whisk or in a blender. Add the greens, cucumbers, and salt. Refrigerate the salad for 25 minutes. Serve cold, sprinkled with chopped walnuts.

Desserts

Armenian Traditional Gata

Preparation time: 60 minutes

Cook time: 30 minutes

Nutrition facts: 1 serving 802 kcal (10g protein, 44g fat, 102g carbs)

Ingredients (10 servings)

21 oz wheat flour

½ teaspoon soda

1 cup sugar icing

¼ cup ghee

2 egg yolk

1 cup butter

½ cup yogurt

Pinch of salt

Preparation

Add 10 oz of flour into a large bowl, add salt and soda. Add butter and mix until crushed. Add yogurt and knead the dough. Put it in a bag or wrap it in a foil and cool it in the refrigerator for 45 minutes. In the meantime, using a mixer, blend the icing sugar with melted butter until it gets white color. Add the remaining flour and mix by hand until a smooth mass is made.

Divide the dough into two parts, roll into a rectangle ¼ inch thick, evenly add half of the filling over the dough, roll the dough into a dense roll. Brush the roll with whipped yolks, make cross-shaped patterns with a fork and cut it into slices of the same size. Repeat the same with the remaining dough and filling. Transfer the *gata* to a baking sheet covered with baking paper and put it in the oven, heated to 400 F for 10 minutes. Reduce the temperature to 360 F and bake for another 20 minutes or until the *gata* is browned. Serve warm.

Pancake Cake with Cottage Cheese and Blueberries

Preparation time: 150 minutes

Nutrition facts: 6 servings: 420 kcal (15g protein, 23g fat, 39g carbs)

Ingredients (6 servings)

11 thin pancakes

15 oz. cottage cheese

1 ½ cup whip cream 35%

2 tablespoon powdered sugar

1 ½ cup blueberry jam

Preparation

Put cottage cheese in bowl and stir well. Whip the whip cream with powdered sugar until thick. Mix cream with cottage cheese, leaving a little to fill the cake on top. Grease each of the 3 pancakes with cream, add blueberries evenly, and repeat this process. Add the remaining cream to the top of the cake. Cool in the refrigerator for at least 60 minutes and then serve.

Curd Bagels with Raspberries

Preparation time: 20 minutes
Cook time: 25 minutes
Nutrition facts: 1 serving 660 kcal (20g protein, 25.9g fat, 99g carbs)

Ingredients (6 servings)

15 oz. curd or cottage cheese

¾ cup butter

2 cups wheat flour

⅓ teaspoon salt

1 cup sugar

1 teaspoon soda

2 teaspoon ground cinnamon

½ cup raspberries

Preparation

Mix oil with cottage cheese. Add flour, soda, and salt. Knead the dough. It should be fairly soft and slightly sticky. Leave in the refrigerator for 30 minutes and then divide it into three parts. Roll each part in turn into a circle with a diameter of 12 inch. Mix the sugar with cinnamon. Sprinkle the rolled dough with part of the mixture. Cut each circle from the center with a knife into 6-12 slices (like pizza). Put 1-2 raspberries on the wide side of each slice and carefully roll from this edge to the inner corner.

Cover the baking sheet with baking paper. Dip the resulting bagel into the remaining mixture of sugar with cinnamon and put sugar on top of the baking sheet. Bake in the oven at 400 F for 20-30 minutes or until the bagels are golden brown. Serve warm.

Armenian Homemade Halva

Preparation time: 60 minutes

Nutrition facts: 1 serving 941 kcal (23g protein, 52g fat, 212g carbs)

Ingredients (4 servings)

2 1/2 cups wheat flour

1 cup ghee

½ cup sugar

¼ cup water

Preparation

Pour the flour into a deep pan and add ghee. Stir until it turns into a crumbly mass of golden color. Add sugar and boiling water and continue stirring until smooth. Put the resulting halva in a mold, cool and serve.

Armenian Traditional Almond Cookies

Preparation time: 20 minutes
Cook time: 45 minutes
Nutrition facts: 1 serving 771 kcal (19g protein, 38g fat, 98.7g carbs)

Ingredients (4 servings)

7 oz wheat flour

15 oz almonds

7 oz sugar

7 oz water

1 egg white

½ cup sugar syrup

Preparation

In a small saucepan, heat the water and then in the pour sugar. Bring the syrup to a boil, stir until the sugar has completely dissolved, and cool slightly. Chop finely half the almonds or melt in the meat grinder and add them as well. Beat the egg whites and, with continuous beating, pour in the syrup. Cook for 15 minutes over low heat, stirring occasionally, and then cool to room temperature.

Gradually introduce flour into this mass and knead the dough for 10 minutes until it becomes consistent. Using a spoon, lay out the dough on a greased and flour-sprinkled baking sheet for a cake. In the center of each cake, add half of the peeled and dried almond kernel. Bake the almond cookies for 25-35 minutes at 360 F, and then refrigerate. Boil the syrup and brush them with cooled cookies.

Quick Custard Cake

Preparation time: 30 minutes

Cook time: 12 minutes

Nutrition facts: 1 serving 821 kcal (13g protein, 36g fat, 112g carbs)

Ingredients (8 servings)

1 1/2 cups sugar

8 1/2 oz butter

4 eggs

2 tablespoon vodka

1 tablespoon honey

1 cup milk

2 teaspoon slaked soda

3 cups wheat flour

Preparation

Dissolve ¼ cup of oil and 1 cup of sugar. Add 3 eggs, 2 tablespoons of vodka into the mass, stir everything, and put in a water bath. Add slaked soda and stir constantly, allowing the mass to increase 3 times. Remove and add 1 tablespoon of honey and flour, so that the dough can be rolled into cakes. Knead the dough and divide into 4 parts. Roll and bake for 3-4 minutes in the oven at 400 F or until golden brown.

Pour milk into a small saucepan and put on fire, add half a cup of sugar, an egg and a tablespoon of flour. Bring to a boil and let cool. Add a cup of oil to the cream. When everything is ready, form the cake itself. Spread cakes one by one and coat with cream. When the cake is ready, trim the uneven edges, and sprinkle the cake on top with any scraps.

Armenian Traditional Baklava

Preparation time: 30 minutes

Cook time: 50 minutes

Nutrition facts: 1 serving 1001kcal (21g protein, 83g fat, 124g carbs)

Ingredients (12 servings)

21 oz walnuts

4-yeast puff pastry

2 cups sugar

6 eggs

2 teaspoon ground cinnamon

6 tablespoon honey

¼ cup butter

Preparation

Separate egg white from the yolk and refrigerate for 15 minutes. Finely chop the nuts with a knife and roll out the dough. Bake two strips of dough at 400 F for 16–22 minutes or until the dough rises and becomes rosy. Then chop the nuts, add a cup of granulated sugar, and cinnamon to them.

Beat the cooled egg white with a mixer. Add a cup of sugar to it and beat again until the bowl is turned upside down and the meringue "stands". Place baking paper on a baking sheet. Smear the meringues. Pour nuts with sugar and cinnamon on top. Cover with a baked strip of dough. Then spread the meringues again, pour the nuts, and cover with a strip of finished dough. And repeat again - on top of meringues and nuts.

Finally, cover the baklava with raw dough, close the edges with fingers. Grease the top with yolk, garnish with walnuts, and put in the oven for 12 minutes.

While the baklava is browning, heat the honey with butter on a stove. Then remove the baklava from the oven, cut it, and gently pour the honey into them. Bake for 28-33 minutes. Baklava is ready for serving!

Almond and Cashew Coffee Cupcake

Preparation time: 15 minutes

Cook time: 42 minutes

Nutrition facts: 1 serving 402 kcal (6g protein, 21g fat, 81g carbs)

Ingredients (10 servings)

½ pound butter

½ pound wheat flour

8 oz sugar

Pinch of salt

3 eggs

1 teaspoon baking powder

2 tablespoon almonds

2 teaspoon roasted cashews

2 tablespoon instant coffee

½ cup chocolate

1 tablespoon cream 10%

6 tablespoon water

Preparation

Beat butter with sugar until a cream is formed. Add eggs and baking powder. Then knead until smooth. Then add 2 tablespoon of instant coffee and pour 6 tablespoons of hot water. Chop the nuts, mix them with coffee, and add to the dough. Mix until smooth. Add the flour. Mix well again.

Put the mixture onto a baking dish. Send it to a preheated oven to 360 F for 32–36 minutes. Meanwhile, break the chocolate and melt in a water bath for 5-7 minutes. Add the remaining cream and coffee to the chocolate. Boil a little. Before serving, pour the icing on the cupcake and decorate with any powder.

Coffee Cake With Curd Cream

Preparation time: 40 minutes

Cook time: 70 minutes

Nutrition facts: 1 serving 659 kcal (14g protein, 41g fat, 88g carbs)

Ingredients (9 servings)

2 ½ cups wheat flour

4 teaspoon instant coffee

2 tablespoon sugar

2/3 teaspoon water

1 ½ teaspoon baking powder

1 teaspoon salt

½ cup vegetable oil

1 teaspoon vanilla

1 dark chocolate

½ teaspoon citric acid

3 cups cream 35%

1 ½ cup sour cream

1 cup soft curd or cottage cheese

6 eggs

½ cup icing sugar

Preparation

Brew coffee in hot water. Grind a bar of chocolate in a grating device. In a large cup, mix the flour, sugar, salt, and baking powder. In the center of the flour mixture, make a hole and pour vegetable oil, egg yolks, coffee and vanilla. Knead well. Add the grated chocolate and knead again.

In a separate cup, beat the egg whites with citric acid. Add to the dough. Gently mix it with a spatula and don't expel the air. Gently line the bottom of the baking dish with parchment. Pour the dough. Bake in the oven, preheated to 360 F for 65–75 minutes. Take it out and leave aside. After cooling, cut into cakes.

Mix the cottage cheese with powdered sugar and sour cream and pierce with a blender to obtain a consistent result. Whip the cream in a separate bowl until soft peaks appear. Carefully combine the curd mixture with whipped cream. Coat the cakes and serve.

Strawberry Orange Dessert with Cardamom Syrup

Preparation time: 15 minutes

Cook time: 15 minutes

Nutrition facts: 1 serving 177 kcal (2.5g protein, 0.8g fat, 37g carbs)

Ingredients (4 servings)

1 ½ cup strawberries

4 oranges

1/3 cup sugar

1/2 cup water

2 cardamom pods

Preparation

Combine sugar, water, and cardamom in a saucepan. Bring to a boil and stir 12-16 minutes or until sugar is dissolved. Remove from heat and let cool. Peel the oranges and carefully cut the segments and transfer to a bowl. Add the sliced strawberries and syrup. Stir well and serve.

Turmeric Cheesecake

Preparation time: 15 minutes

Cook time: 6 minutes

Nutrition facts: 2 servings: 277 kcal (12g protein, 16,5g fat, 37g carbs)

Ingredients (4 servings)

3 tablespoon wheat flour

½ teaspoon turmeric

1 egg

1 teaspoon sugar

½ cup semolina

1 teaspoon ghee

1 cup cottage cheese

1 cup curd weight

Preparation

Grind the egg with sugar and then add flour and turmeric. Combine the resulting mass with cottage cheese and curd mass. Using hands, moistened with water, form 8 cheesecakes, and roll in semolina and flour. Fry in a preheated frying pan in ghee for 3 minutes on each side.

Cheesecakes with Dried Apricots and Walnuts

Preparation time: 15 minutes

Cook time: 5 minutes

Nutrition facts: 1 serving: 621 kcal (21g protein, 17g fat, 67g carbs)

Ingredients (4 servings)

7 oz. curd or cottage cheese

2 tablespoon wheat flour

1 tablespoon semolina

2 tablespoon sugar

1 egg

2 tablespoon powdered sugar

¼ cup dried apricots

¼ cup walnuts

3 tablespoon vegetable oil

Preparation

Soak the dried apricots in water. Rub the cottage cheese through a sieve and add sugar, egg, sifted flour, and semolina. Mix. Chop walnuts and dried apricots and add to the dough. Roll the dough and cut it into circles. Heat the oil in a pan, add the cheesecakes, and fry on each side for 2 minutes. Put them on a plate and sprinkle with powdered sugar.

Traditional Armenian Drinks

Lemonade with Tarragon

Preparation time: 20 minutes

Nutrition facts: 1 serving 121 kcal (1g protein, 0.1g fat, 53g carbs)

Ingredients

3 tablespoon tarragon

2 lemon

¾ cup sugar syrup

5 cups sparkling water

Preparation

Finely chop the tarragon. Squeeze the juice from the lemons. Mix the lemon juice with the sugar syrup. Drain half of sparkling water from the bottle. Put the tarragon into the bottle. Pour the syrup and tightly close the lid, let the lemonade brew in the refrigerator for at least 20 minutes. Strain the lemonade through a sieve and serve in glasses.

Armenian Traditional Drink-Syrup (*Mulberry Doshab*)

Cook time: 120 minutes

Nutrition facts: 1 serving 95 kcal (1g protein, 7g fat, 92g carbs)

Ingredients (10 servings)

2 cups water

10 pounds white mulberry

Preparation

Cook on the berries of the mulberry on a very small fire for 70 minutes after boiling. Filter everything under pressure. Pour juice into a wide bowl and boil over low heat for another 70 minutes. Remove the foam while cooking. If the foam stops appearing, the juice will be dark and the *doshab* is ready for serving.

Armenian Kampari Drink

Preparation time: 10 minutes

Nutrition facts: 1 serving 219kcal (9g protein, 16g fat, 45g carbs)

Ingredients

¼ cup Armenian grape wine

¼ cup Campari

¼ cup sparkling water

½ teaspoon almond powder

4 ice cubes

Preparation

Take a huge glass and add all ingredients together. Mix well with a spoon and serve.

Armenian Atlama

Preparation time: 5 minutes

Nutrition facts: 1 serving 91 kcal (3.2g protein, 1g fat, 72g carbs)

Ingredients (4 servings)

2 cups Armenian Yogurt (*matsun*)

2 cups sparkling water

1 cucumber

½ bunch basil

2 bunch green onions

Salt to taste

Preparation

Chop all of the ingredients, then add to the blender for 2 minutes, and serve with ice cubes.

Tarragon Drink

Preparation time: 30 minutes

Nutrition facts: 1 serving 51kcal (2g protein, 0g fat, 41g carbs)

Ingredients (2 servings)

2 oz tarragon leaves

2 cups water

1 lemon

1 lime

1 tablespoon sugar

2 teaspoon honey

Preparation

Cut the tarragon leaves and add 2 cups of boiling water on it. Then add all remaining ingredients and cool it in the fridge for 40 minutes.

Strawberry Matsun Shake

Preparation time: 5 minutes
Nutrition facts: 1 serving 102 kcal (4g protein, 1,2g fat, 32g carbs)

Ingredients

¼ cup milk
¼ cup Armenian yogurt (*matsun*)
¼ cup strawberry puree
2 tablespoon cinnamon syrup
4 ice cubes
A slice of mango for decoration

Preparation

Stir milk, *matsun*, and the strawberry puree in the blender for 2 minutes. Add cinnamon syrup, ice and mix together in a blender for an additional 2 minutes. Garnish with a leaf of mint or a slice of mango.

Akroshka

Preparation time: 5 minutes

Nutrition facts: 1 serving 102 kcal (4g protein, 1,2g fat, 32g carbs)

Ingredients (2 servings)

½ cup Armenian yogurt (*matsun*)

¼ cup sour cream

½ cucumber

1 ½ oz mixed greens

4 ice cubes

1 cup of water

1 teaspoon salt

Preparation

In a jar add *matsun*, sour cream, and a teaspoon of salt. Cut the cucumber and mixed greens and add into the jar. While stirring, add a cup of water, ice cubes, and serve.

Sauces

Armenian Barbecue Sauce

Preparation time: 5 minutes

Cook time: 10 minutes

Nutrition facts: 1 serving 121 kcal (7g protein, 1g fat, 23g carbs)

Ingredients (4 servings)

1 bunch fresh cilantro

1 can tomato paste

1 cup water

1 garlic clove

1 bunch basil

1 onion

1 teaspoon salt

Ground black pepper pinch

Preparation

Dilute the tomato paste with water on a medium heat for 6 minutes or until the mixture boils. Add finely chopped onions, herbs, spices, and garlic. Cook for another 6 minutes. Let it cool well and serve.

Herb Marinade with Herbs and Lemon Zest

Preparation time: 125 minutes

Nutrition facts: 1 serving 167kcal (2g protein, 11g fat, 10,8g carbs)

Ingredients (5 servings)

2 tablespoons olive oil

2 tablespoon fresh chopped rosemary

2 tablespoon ground sage leaves

2 tablespoon balsamic vinegar

2 tablespoon shredded fresh thyme

4 cloves of garlic

1 lemon

Preparation

Grate the lemon zest on a fine grater and transfer to a bowl. Add olive oil, rosemary, sage, thyme, and chopped garlic. Mix well. Put the meat previously prepared into the mold, pour the marinade, close and keep in the refrigerator for 130 minutes.

Sun-Dried Tomato Sauce

Preparation time: 20 minutes
Cook time: 30 minutes
Nutrition facts: 1 serving 429 kcal (11g protein, 28g fat, 40,1g carbs)

Ingredients (5 servings)

7 red chili pepper
1 teaspoon cumin seeds (*zira*)
1 teaspoon ground coriander
1 tablespoon tomato paste
4 cloves of garlic
2 tablespoons olive oil
3 sun-dried tomatoes in oil
Salt to taste

Preparation

Preheat oven to 360 F. Bake chili pepper for 25 minutes or until bubbles form, without covering. Remove from the oven, peel, remove the seeds and stalks. In a mortar, crush the seeds of *zira*, chop the garlic finely, and combine. Add coriander, sun-dried tomatoes, tomato paste, and salt. Process everything in a blender until a fairly uniform paste is obtained.

Armenian Meat Sauce

Preparation time: 10 minutes
Cook time: 16 minutes
Nutrition facts: 1 serving 136 kcal (1g protein, 4g fat, 20g carbs)

Ingredients (4 servings)
¾ cup dried black figs
1 ½ teaspoon coarse salt
1 teaspoon tomato paste
¼ cup balsamic vinegar
2 teaspoon sunflower oil
2 cloves of garlic
1 bay leaf
3 cups of water

Preparation
Put the figs in a bowl, pour 2 cups of boiling water, and leave for 5 minutes. Drain and transfer to a blender. Add vinegar, tomato paste and 1 teaspoon of salt. Beat until smooth. Heat the sunflower oil in a saucepan over medium heat. Add the chopped garlic and fry for 30 seconds. Then add the fig mass, 1 cup of water, and a bay leaf. Cook on low heat for 15 minutes, salt, and remove the bay leaf. Serve.

Walnut Adjika

Preparation time: 40 minutes
Nutrition facts: 1 servings 77kcal (2g protein, 5g fat, 19g carbs)

Ingredients (20 servings)

2 cups red chili

1 ½ cups garlic

1 cup walnuts

2 teaspoon *khmeli suneli* (or similar spice)

1 ½ teaspoon salt

Preparation

Cut the stalks from the peppers but leave the seeds. Put peppers, peeled garlic, and nuts through a meat grinder, add all the spices, and process well. Squeeze the resulting mass through a cheesecloth to get rid of excess juice. Transfer adjika to a jar and store in the refrigerator for 40 minutes.

If you liked Armenian food, discover to how cook DELICIOUS recipes from other Balkan countries!

Within these pages, you'll learn 35 authentic recipes from a Balkan cook. These aren't ordinary recipes you'd find on the Internet, but recipes that were closely guarded by our Balkan mothers and passed down from generation to generation.

Main Dishes, Appetizers, and Desserts included!

If you want to learn how to make Croatian green peas stew, and 32 other authentic Balkan recipes, then start with our book!

Order <u>HERE</u> now for only $2,99

If you're a Mediterranean dieter who wants to know the secrets of the Mediterranean diet, dieting, and cooking, then you're about to discover how to master cooking meals on a Mediterranean diet right now!

In fact, if you want to know how to make Mediterranean food, then this new e-book - "The 30-minute Mediterranean diet" - gives you the answers to many important questions and challenges every Mediterranean dieter faces, including:

- How can I succeed with a Mediterranean diet?
- What kind of recipes can I make?
- What are the key principles to this type of diet?
- What are the suggested weekly menus for this diet?
- Are there any cheat items I can make?

... and more!

If you're serious about cooking meals on a Mediterranean diet and you really want to know how to make Mediterranean food, then you need to grab a copy of "The 30-minute Mediterranean diet" right now.

Prepare **111 recipes with several ingredients in less than 30 minutes!**

Order <u>HERE</u> now for only $2,99!

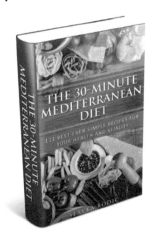

What could be better than a home-cooked meal? Maybe only a Greek homemade meal.

Do not get discouraged if you have no Greek roots or friends.

Now you can make a Greek food feast in your kitchen.

This ultimate Greek cookbook offers you 111 best dishes of this cuisine! From more famous gyros to more exotic Kota Kapama this cookbook keeps it easy and affordable.

All the ingredients necessary are wholesome and widely accessible.

The author's picks are as flavorful as they are healthy. The dishes described in this cookbook are "what Greek mothers have made for decades."

Full of well-balanced and nutritious meals, this handy cookbook includes many vegan options.
Discover a plethora of benefits of Mediterranean cuisine, and you may fall in love with cooking at home.

Inspired by a real food lover, this collection of delicious recipes will taste buds utterly satisfied.

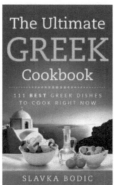

Order at Amazon for only $2,99!

Maybe to try exotic Serbian cuisine?

From succulent sarma, soups, warm and cold salads to delectable desserts, the plethora of flavors will satisfy the most jaded foodie. Have a taste of a new culture with this **traditional Serbian cookbook**.

Order at Amazon for only $2,99!

Maybe to try some Persian cuisine?

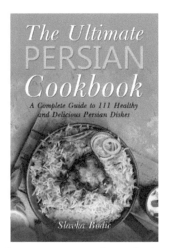

Order <u>HERE</u> now for only $2,99!

One Last Thing

I f you enjoyed this book or found it useful I'd be very grateful if you could find the time to post a short review on Amazon. Your support really does make a difference and I read all the reviews personally, so I can get your feedback and make this book even better.

Thanks again for your support!

Please send me your feedback at

www.balkanfood.org

Made in United States
Troutdale, OR
09/21/2023

13091106R00094